HOME TRUTHS

A collection of poetry

Philip John

WORDCATCHER publishing

Home Truths
Wordcatcher Modern Poetry

© 2018 Philip John
Source images supplied by Adobe Stock
Cover design © 2018 David Norrington

The Author asserts the moral right to be identified as the author of this work. All rights reserved. This book is protected under the copyright laws of the United Kingdom. Any reproduction or other unauthorised use of the material or artwork herein is prohibited without the express written permission of the Publisher.

No part of this book may be reproduced, stored in a retrieval system, or transmitted in any form or by any means, electronic, electrostatic, magnetic tape, mechanical, photocopying, recording or otherwise, without the written permission of the Publisher.

British Library Cataloguing in Publication Data.
A catalogue record for this book is available from the British Library.

Published in the United Kingdom by Wordcatcher Publishing Group Ltd
www.wordcatcher.com
Tel: 02921 888321
Facebook.com/WordcatcherPublishing

First Edition: 2018

Print edition ISBN: 9781789420531
Ebook edition ISBN: 9781789420524

Category: Poetry

There are people and places that will be with me forever.
Many of them are in this book.

Contents

Part Three

Part One

A Beautiful World

Reincarnation

Rolling, tumbling at the water's edge,
Black lambs suckling on the whitest sheep,
The gatherer of daffodils sheds tears for the travellers,
As the intrepid move on and the world goes by.

Standing atop the mountains,
Where the weeds move upward,
And the rocks crumble into dust,
Blown by the wind toward the beaten track,
A rusted red gate promises the wanderers of the adventures of
    the past.

Sanctuary found in the fountains of the forgotten,
The quiet chords of birdsong floating in the air,
And just for a fleeting moment,
You were never really there.

Paradise

An unrelenting golden blanket,
Broken only by the invitation of the white horses.
One for the drifters and the dreamers,
This is it. Paradise.

Strangers walk on,
Warming their hearts in the midday sun.
Beating drums only soften to the sound of the colours,
Vibrant as the fruit of kindness,
And as sweet as Heaven's punch.

The Wood

The honey bees,
Swept up in the green,
Just like me.
And from a magic dance,
It settles in this wood.

My friend runs free,
His coat of brown at one,
With the bark of every tree.
The inquisitor of horses,
And all around the cows,
He passes by the stream,
To quench a thirsty quest.

In all the years, rain or shine,
In this wood, the world is mine.

The Heart of the Valley

The heart of the valley is beating below,
Hidden in the hills where clear rivers flow,
The blackest of pits from days gone by,
Voices of men who are lost in time.

The heart of the valley is beating below,
Where choirs of children filled chapels with song,
Forests of freedom,
A place you belong.

The heart of the valley is beating below,
Row upon row of boxes fill the void.
Humble and hungry,
What is that noise?
The beat goes on,
But for how long?

People of passion and spirit remain,
The heart of the valley is not beating in vein,
The fire still burns in the mountains,
The dragon is waiting within.

The Magnificent Mountains

The curator of the magnificent mountains,
Is a deeper shade of blue.
Washing the sands of a dreaming shore,
Life ascends into a pocket of unquenchable rainbows.

Lilies splash the valley,
And the air melts the hungry hearts.
The scent of a sweet wine,
And the feast of Kings,
Passes through the hands.
The villages are singing,
A living, breathing work of art.

As the ships settle on a willing tide,
Memories made and locked inside,
They sail away,
Still warm from the afternoon glow,
Quietly slipping through.
Soon to return to search again,
For the secrets buried deep within.

Faraway

Eastern skies are a different night,
A shepherd of the faraway places.
These market streets burned by the moon,
Spreading wide and spiralling high,
Mesmerising lights,
The wonder inside.

Hustle and dust, rising up.
No time to lose but for a bite,
I stop amidst the storm,
And chop through another delight.
Place of exotic aroma,
Smoky, succulent all over,
My romance.

Take me through the town,
Show me what you know.
I'm faraway, you're home.

The Waterfront

In that indifferent afternoon,
In the shade of a lonely bar,
Sat at an only table,
Sipping a golden nectar.

It was a gentle breeze that fed the wry smile,
And a still bay of palisades,
Waved the fond farewell.

Light Years

I went on a journey, middle of the night,
To the end of the world, no Earth in sight.
A spiral of memories,
Fighting for their place to rest,
Pouring out of the nothingness,
A crying luminescence.

I went a bit further, to the edge of all that had ever been,
I spoke with the masters and walked with the Gods,
There were no answers and there was no truth,
Only a flux of fluid, spilling from the mouth of the universe.

I made my way back, later that night,
Met the descendants of the interstellar men,
Who launched themselves across the galaxy,
In search of new worlds, innocent and free.
But only sun-kissed chaos and arctic emptiness,
With sinister sentinels presiding those realms.

I returned from my journey at the end of the night,
When the weary red fox made for the den,
And above, the beginning of a song from a wren.
I watched the sun rise up from beneath the sea,
Nowhere else I'd rather be.

Back to Life

A wander through my own museum,
Talking to the ghosts of happiness.
The edge of the cliff looks just the same,
And the house on the hill endures.
Walking the path of a forgotten coast,
Calming the waters before the storm.
Life is twisting, turning,
But here is a place that brings you back.
Back into the world,
And back to life.

The Grand Design

You cannot see the spectres of yesterday,
Or the unwritten pages of tomorrow,
Not from inside this marble prison,
But from a twitch in the curtain,
I know there is more than meets the eye.

What can we conjure up,
A small, troubled mind in an infinite universe,
A Sentient in waiting.
The shadow moves across the glass,
Breathing a sigh from the other side,
Or just a salsa of smoke,
Dancing across the mirror to the soul.

Turning the pages of the grand design,
As the passerine songs enchant,
Bronzed crabs fade away across the moonlit path,
To the world and all its pearls.
The harp in the stars plays an ancient rhyme as old as the sky,
Holding on,
Another song before the dawn,
One more dance for life.

Until the End

Clandestine embers falling through the sky,
Anything but faded dreams shall die.
Vast and impossible, a waterfall of time,
Whispers of the past drowning in the silence.
In beautiful fragility, it shatters and crumbles,
No trace or shadow left in its wake,
The future unwritten, ready to break.

How can it be so pure,
But engulfed in the dark.
An earthly pearl wrapped in its oceans,
So little and so much,
All we can see and all we can touch.

If for a moment and at a glance,
The Gods descend for the final dance,
I can see the falling fire drop into the water,
Thinking not of how it came to be,
Basking in its glory,
From now until the end.

Last Day on Earth

No sense of occasion or finality,
Just broken minds and aching hearts,
My Earth is beautiful,
But nothing ever lasts.

We made it, you see,
The ones that came down from the trees,
And built a world, it was civilisation.
Who knew then that it would always be,
Its very own downfall and mortality.

And if you want to see it on the final day,
Let me show you,
The finest place in the galaxy,
Where the oceans swallow the sun at night,
Replaced by that silver coin in the sky.
I'll take you to a land of emerald dreams,
Where, born from the smallest acorns,
Oak trees stand tall and endure,
A mighty tomb for the end of a rich life.
From the deserts paved with gold,
To the ravishing glaciers, a heaven to behold.

Then I'll show you where we made our mark,
The cathedrals of masterpiece,
And the towering works of art.
The castles in my mountains,
A gallery of conquest,
From a long and distant past.

Now that spring has sprung,
And the swallows they have sung,
I'll take you down to the sandy bay,
'Neath a cliff touching clouds at the break of day.
When that sun sinks one more time,
You will know of all my love,
For the wonder of my world,
The greatest wonder in all the universe.

Part Two

War and Peace

An Unconquerable Tongue

Red wings that carried them,
Far along a solitary shore,
Where the Princes of Gwynedd had gathered before.
The bittersweet lifeblood,
And an unconquerable tongue,
The real treasure.

Magicians in the mountains,
Under the spell of a colonial craze,
Carrying the cost through a hellish, bloody maze.

Eternal rebellion,
Transcending the myth and forefathers' legend.
The last man standing shall not shake the hand,
Nor break his oath to his father's land.
His final, unhindered swindle,
Relentless and unforgiving,
Lay it to rest but forget me not.

Only we could remember,
The bloodshed and selfless sacrifice,
As we were beaten out of words,
Given unto us by the brave warriors,
Who would not fall in the face of defeat.
Carry we did,
A language of unquestionable immortality,
Through all adversity,
And into the light.

The Gallery of Time

The gallery of time washed up on this desolate shore,
Evoking the demons that are certain to have walked this Earth
    before.
Men of honour, men of the hour,
Blood will boil, hearts will sour.

Chambers of truth locked in mortality,
Death is thy neighbour,
The only reality.

Look over yonder,
Horizon of hope,
No time to wonder,
Ponder amidst the thunder,
Sudden and sodden,
A leader's blunder.

If you shall not walk this Earth again,
Know you have died a hero,
Remembered for them.

Old Man, Young Man

In the dusty plains of chaos,
Fighting for the lie,
The freedom of man.
In the scorched and barren lands,
Here I am,
Young man,
Blood on my hands.

The comrades march together,
Brothers in the desert.
As the sun sets in the undead sky,
The shots slice the air.
Facing the enemy for one last time,
To win your game,
For your fortune and fame.
There you are,
Old Man,
Who's blood is on your hands?

Raging on, all systems go,
Satan was sleeping in a mine just below.
One last flash,
Flesh flies above,
And death descends.
Here I am,
Young man,
My Brother's blood in my hands.

Victory

The furnace of fear burns deep within,
Walking through the pantheon,
Judged by all that walked before,
But glory was not made in that moment,
It was built by the battered hands and etched from the rugged
    stone.

When the fortress is ready to hold the dragon before the flight,
When the mighty have fallen and death has abided the heroes,
You will walk free from the forest,
Free from the gateway of the guardians,
Where it will be found.
Not framed in gold nor held upon the top of the world,
But standing and staring at all that is left,
When victory is yours.

Equinox

A flame and tomb of paper moths,
A sweet honey running wild,
A nameless footbridge from here to there,
A magpie on a fragile branch,
A handwritten letter with dribbling ink,
Words running away in autumn showers.
Words of all the friends and lovers,
Recalling the days that never end.

The Lady Across the Room

Eyes so wide but with room to spare,
Written in that momentary stare,
Born from a weary smile,
Exploding from within,
Just like marigold in full bloom,
That was the lady across the room.

Time slipped away with nothing to show,
Another dropped stitch in an unfinished tapestry,
Onwards and upwards,
What it means to be free.

And as it came to pass,
Autumn leaves falling on the grass,
The world moved again without a second's glance.

The phoenix waited in the wings,
Perched up on high,
Gazing across the golden forests,
The end was nigh.

At the closing of just another day,
The darkness descended and the phoenix rose,
Burning through the heart,
Touching the soul.

Butterfly

In the earthly springs I find my place,
Not far from a heavenly plane.
Eluding the grasp of a heady hand,
I fly on the whispers of a bewildered child.

Precious in flight and precarious on foot,
Wonderful and delicate,
A ripple through the harp.
Don't look for me,
Don't follow me.

When the blood falls on the forgotten sky,
I will rest upon your shoulder,
Your happiness,
Your butterfly.

In the Suburb of a Dead Town

The lonely streets are quiet tonight,
As the moon gladly tells of the times gone by.
Because he's seen it all,
From the birth of the Queen's rock,
To the warring of the Ancient tribes.
But the sleepy houses are tired now,
In the suburb of a dead town.

The rising sun can tell you more,
Of man and boy setting sail for the foreign shore,
To fight in someone else's war.
Of man and boy breaking their backs,
To dig and dig for the diamonds of black.
Mothers, like rocks, holding the fort,
The struggle for freedom waging on.

The place has not lost its voice,
But does not speak of the mystery,
Of this beautiful land,
Steeped in history.
Nothing left to prove,
As I walk atop the rolling green hills,
Staring down,
In the suburb of a dead town.

The Champion

In the darkest of days,
When the rot is killing the root,
Keep on digging.

In the deepest of oceans,
When life is drowning in the waves,
Keep on swimming.

In the harshest desert,
When the sun has purged the land of all its green,
Keep on walking.

Against a sea of vagrant wanderers,
Misguided by the flashing lights,
Do not turn,
Do not look back.

For the noble move forward, always.
When the fire of fury wages war inside,
And all pathways lead to another horizon,
The champion remains,
With scars and sorrows,
But stronger,
Stronger than ever before.

Living in my Dreams

In a hazy winter's dream,
The cold falls softly upon the night.
In the wonderland, she is calling.

Lost in eternal freedom,
Those memories of a sacred sanctuary,
Holding me tightly.
The voice is pure and unbroken,
An angel living in my dreams,
I have asked and you have spoken.

Before the fading black restores the slumber,
And I slip away,
The door never closes,
Not even at the break of day.

Lost and Found

In the corner of all the darkness,
There is everything to be found.
As it is when the man is most lost,
There is everything to be won.

The walk into that world might suck the life,
And wrestle with the truth,
But being there is a battle alone,
A battle fought by the weary soldier.

Rising up slowly with almost nothing left,
And a lasting stare up at the midnight haze,
Tells of all that needs to be said.
Wherever you are tonight,
We stand and share the same moonlight.

Where the Heart Is

A walk out in the world again,
All it takes,
The smell of home in the street,
And it's not so different anymore.

The lost and the found,
And I know now,
However upside down it gets,
After life's trauma,
And out of the clutches of chaos,
I can go back to this place.
I am this place.
My rock, my heart.

Part Three

Home Truths

The Age of Convenience

The age of convenience has brought upon me,
An increasing sense of worldwide apathy.
God is a screen and heaven is in cyberspace,
Plugged in but logged off,
The system is your saving grace.
The world is connected in every which way,
Except for the souls of a crying generation,
Cold from the waves of the sonic boom.
All of us out there for a quick fix,
Expert knowledge... is it really just a click?

That on your plate, ready in a flash,
Filling your face with no time to last.
The factory's slaughter in your hands,
Is profit for the system and profit for the man.
Listen to the screaming sound of starvation,
Are you still hungry or in need of education?

Don't moderate just medicate, vegetate,
Drink it dry and in full measure,
Trade future pain for instant pleasure.
Living with our heads deep beneath the plains,
In goldfish bowls of happiness,
It's driving me insane.

Keep lighting the fuse that fuels the world,
Chasing the mirage of happiness,
In a rainbow of fire and smoke,
Melting the lungs and suffocating the ocean,
The Mother has spoken...
"You have the answers in the palm of your hands."

Take a walk into the wilderness,
The birds are still singing to us,
And the land is still alive.
Fight to break new ground before the ground has broken,
Fight to see the sunrise after the final dawn.
The age of convenience has brought upon me,
A time for change and a new frontier.

Food for Thought

Battered, fried and dressed to impress,
Lining your stomachs with a bloody mess.
No question of who it was and how it lived,
Just another course in a fully stacked fridge.
Remorseless waste and extra large waists,
Bought and paid for by the human disgrace.

Detached from reality in an ignorant bliss,
The starving would give anything for just a bit of this.
It matters not to those comfortable creatures,
The great unwashed and the guilty preachers.
Not the only ones to blame,
In a corrupted commercial game.
Blinded from the truth by a marketing dream,
Where everything sourced is ethical and free,
Pumped and packaged just for you and me,
To fill ourselves up on another's misery.
Consuming the world, mouthfuls at a time,
In nature's trial, guilty of all crimes.

Where is the fight for sustainability?
Make this a world of giving and reciprocity,
Don't replace it with a footprint of regret,
Not too far down that road yet.

Organic

The fabric of my faculties,
Threadbare as the worn out carpet,
To an old coal fire,
Burning through the night.

I washed away the toil,
In a rustic and rusted tin,
Somewhere in that simplicity,
I was whole, free from sin.

The Devil's Currency

Too many lives devoted,
To the Devil's currency,
Consumers are hunting,
They are hungry.

Fuelled by a fashionable dream,
With the underbelly of a dying stream.
Synthetic meals and fraudulent deals,
Beneath the smile is a deep, deep misery.

Filling the bags of plastic,
With substitutes for contentment,
They know not what they do.
For not many miles away,
The bags are infesting the waters,
And the marauders of the urban streets,
Go without again tonight.

The masters of the golden bank,
Play God with the sorry folk,
The eternal quest for self-perfection,
A dangerous obsession.
Is the inner self lost in the past?
Or dying a slow, painful death?

What becomes of sold souls,
Who lost themselves long ago.
Only time will tell,
If they can ever break free,
From an irreparable spell.

If only they would awaken,
And open themselves a door to truth,
A stark revelation,
But perhaps a pathway,
A pathway to real happiness.

In Sickness and In Health

There's an epidemic,
Spreading like the wildest fire.
Turning the back on those cast iron barbells,
To sit down beside a mirror, barely breaking a sweat,
And without the real fuel of desire.
The goal is just a cosmetic perfection,
From a library of pharmaceutical affliction.
Diet plans and disappointment,
Blinding you with scientific fiction,
Because you need to believe,
That the answers lie with someone else.
Someone other than yourself.

Back to the basics can't be enough,
Let's pay for something that looks the part,
Unlimited calories and fat reducing pills,
That's got to be the answer to a healthy heart.

Complicated strategies and expert dialogue,
Spellbinding supplements in extra special packaging.
It's a failure to face reality and the very simple truth,
A little balance and a little discipline,
Goes the longest way,
To a healthy and happy life.

Redemption

A bag on the back, skin on the bone,
It's life in the gutter from a suburban throne.
A shadow of all that promise,
A beggar and a thief,
Penny for your thoughts,
Never will it drop.
The rock is not even the bottom,
Temptation not a pleasure,
Not even a desire,
Just a way of life.

No sign of a little warmth,
And compassion came with no receipt,
Out there on the dead streets.
Tired of this game,
Borrowed in vein,
Buried in the shame.

It's been a long time now,
Many nights on the fringes,
Getting by like a natural,
Getting high on collateral.
In that bitter Autumn drizzle,
Like a hammer falling upon the final nail,
A hand reached out,
And then it never felt the same.

A home that warmed the heart by its open fire,
No words to be said,
Just a hot broth shared,
In an unsung moment.
That was the night that raised the dead.

It's been a longer time now,
With little ground covered,
It could be said.
But it was a long way back,
Inside the head,
In a place that few have ever escaped.

A Glass of Fortune

A glass of fortune, drink of choice,
It's the gambler's time to make his mark.
Spinning the wheels that race through life,
Men of the highest order,
Falling on down with the Devil's bite.

Numbers floating through the air,
Rolling dice without a care,
Marching on to the beat of the drum,
All you own is all you have won.

Wrapped in a storm after one last spin,
The house is the one with the final grin.
Look around you,
At all that is left,
All you ever needed,
Not a glass of fortune, guilty as sin,
Breaking even feels like a win.

No more tricks up the sleeve,
Time to stop, to breathe.
Folding the hand before the lonely walk home,
The gambling man has a long way to go.
Stack the odds and hang the head,
The headstone waits for the name,
Of the lucky man that played one more game.

Secrets in the head, the demon is unleashed.
Walking free and out of the fold,
If you drink a glass of fortune, beware,
And don't make it too bold.

The Nature of the Beast

Who holds the key to the secret of our dreams?
The puppet master just feeds the beast,
And the soldiers on the ground are fighting,
Not for the good of the West or the might of the East,
But just so the game goes on.

Whilst the hungry vultures send the world up in smoke,
The desperate cry out against the nature of the beast,
The beast that bought them a dream,
Sold them a promise,
With no receipt and no guarantee.

The cogs in the wheel who once worked for a pittance,
Are working still but for maybe a little more,
Winding the gears with a greener mind,
Can we save ourselves or are we out of time?

Black Gold

A sickened society,
Running a crude fever,
The age of oil is a means to an end,
The end.

Muddy the waters with a corporate smile,
Bury the ashes of the forest,
Singed and trampled just for me and you.
Life in salt waters filled with the empties,
Smothered in a plastic sea.
The smog crawls into young lungs,
Blackening the breath,
Crying for what's left.

Time for the mother's medicine,
The cure is in the treasure,
A treasure already ours.
The waves that gift the world with life,
And the sun and its powers that be.
Catching the wind that shakes the sky,
The home of the wild; released and free.
The green lungs intact,
Breathing freshly again.
The war for black gold,
Soon to be just a story of old.
The door can only be held for so long,
When the elements awaken,
We can make it there.

Renewable Me

It doesn't make a difference,
If it doesn't make a difference,
There is a simple pleasure,
In a renewable me.

My footprint melts in the breeze,
I'm only taking what I really need.
Not wanting, never wasting,
It's collective and reciprocal,
It should all be cyclical.
And I want you to know,
That I think of you,
Each time that I do.

Lost Boy

Oh lost boy,
So many miles from your quiet home,
How will you survive,
In the apocalypse of a neon jungle,
I'm thinking of you now,
Wherever you may roam.

If you can stay to build your dreams,
In the noise of the industrial thunder,
And through the thick black smoke,
And the flashing signs of compromise,
You can find yourself in there,
In the darkest of days,
When home is calling deep within your heart.

Some day you will return,
Even if for a passing moment in time,
And then you will return a man.
A man who knows the secret,
To see the world in all its glory.
From those resting deep beneath the earth,
Up to the sky full of dancing stars.
Stars that fill the soul with majesty.

Visitors

Who is that man with the dusty boxes?
Surging on and breaking the back of the lonely donkey.

Who is that girl with hopeful eyes?
Crying out for just a little more.

Who is that baby in a young woman's arms?
With an old rag under a battered tin roof for shade.

Who is that boy staring back at the simple life?
He's wondering just how it came to be.

Who is that man staring back?
The man from the west,
With his electronic tools and brand new shoes.

Exchanging but a token and a smile,
A glass of kindness can last a long time.
Some day they might return,
When the man and the donkey are long gone,
And the boy is a man singing a different kind of song.

Colour Blind

Life through a lens of black and white,
An imitation of those that were living,
In the mausoleum of the mind.

Pictures of me,
Pictures of you,
Tired of the colours,
Tired of the blue.
There's something in the way you talk,
That tells me the best is yet to come.
Your whisper is carried through my skin,
And every lonesome night,
The closer to the bone.

In the window is the light of tomorrow,
For all the days and nights that pass,
The more I want to see,
Of all the colours,
That you can bring to me.

Strange Days

Who is really free,
In a managed democracy?
The caricatures fight for their place,
As the figurehead of the human race.

A preferred propaganda controls the new age,
All this anger is all the rage.
The master plan is firmly in place,
One fake news story and your life is a disgrace.
An online presence for offline minds,
Sure to appeal to the impressionable kind.
Big screen, little screen,
Headlines and sound bites,
Get the masses behind the masters,
So the unfortunate few won't have a clue.

Dictators or leaders, the angle is acute,
A cold-hearted smile and a three piece suit.
You might get them to confess it,
A risky vote and a slow, painful exit.
Strange days are indeed upon us,
A roll of the dice,
A shuffle of the deck,
The only card that might trump your own,
Has already been dealt.

Keep believing and stay inspired,
For the faithful shall be called upon.
Not taking these strange days with brute or force,
But with time, tact and self-preservation,
The saviour is coming,
It's the next generation.

Freedom

A simple life it is to live in harmony,
Taking from the mother only what we need,
And planting again to sow the seeds.
The footprint of man need not be heavy,
Another trail is almost afoot,
And the path is less travelled no longer.

Take the land and sea,
Take the world,
Be free.

Innocence

Untouched by the weight of a heavy world,
Before the first, fatal kiss,
In the grand old garden, the closest to bliss.
Stood in a street so familiar,
The only one that may have ever been.
I was lost picking berries,
Then falling through the ferns,
In a forever place.

Faces I know, I love,
They turn with the ticking of the hand.
Holy houses fall through the seasons,
And I lament.
I lament for all that was promised is lost,
Though it stayed for long enough,
Until friends had flown,
And wise old mentors had resigned.

And as the world around decays,
So do people, and time itself.
But slow enough to savour,
Every ember of youth.

WORDCATCHER publishing

Poetry Series

Visit **www.wordcatcher.com**
to discover new voices and classic poetry.

We also publish:

History
Business
Politics

Real Life and True Stories

Short Story Collections and Anthologies
Historical Fiction
Crime & Thrillers
Literary Fiction
Humour

Creative Portfolios by
Authors, Illustrators, Artists, and other Creative Talent

Spoken Emotion

A collection of poetry about adoption

ELIZABETH & OLIVER ARCHER

Cycles

A collection of Haiku poetry

JOE WOODHOUSE

Blunt Force
A Collection of Poetry

GARY BECK

Lightning Source UK Ltd.
Milton Keynes UK
UKHW040940080219

336898UK00001B/152/P